The Farmer Who Went Out To Sow

AMERICAN BIBLE SOCIETY
NEW YORK

The Farmer Who Went Out To Sow (Vol. 12)
Scripture quotes from the *Contemporary English Version,* Matthew 13.1-9 (CEV).
Wording and grammar represent the kind of language best understood
and appreciated by young readers.

Copyright © 1995, American Bible Society
1865 Broadway, New York, N. Y. 10023
www.americanbible.org

Illustrations by Chantal Muller van den Berghe
Text by Bernard Hubler and Claude-Bernard Costecalde, Ph. D.
Design by Jacques Rey

Copyright © 1997, Éditions du Signe
Strasbourg, France

ISBN 1-58516-177-2
Printed in Italy
Eng. Port. CEV 560 P - 109869
ABS - 7/00 - 5,000

Sometimes, when Jesus wanted to get his message
across to the men and women of his time, he used
a type of story called a "parable".
These stories work not only for the people of Jesus' time,
but also for the people of all time, and places.
So his message is for us too in our day.
How can we begin to understand what this message
is all about?
Once, Jesus compared God's word to a seed,
which a farmer plants, all over his land.
The seed bears fruit if it falls in good soil.

That same day Jesus left the house and went out beside Lake Galilee, where he sat down to teach.

Jesus did a lot of teaching.
That was part of his mission.
He often did it by the side of the lake
and when there were large crowds
he got into a boat.
So that people would understand him
better he compared one thing
with another, using stories
that are called "parables".

*When we have an image, a picture
or a comparison, we can understand things better.*

"A farmer went out to sow seed in a field."

Jesus told the crowd,
"A farmer went out to sow seed in a field."
Everyone knew what he was talking about:
the farmer putting his hand into the bag
which hung around his neck,
taking a fistful of seed and scattering
it all over the place.

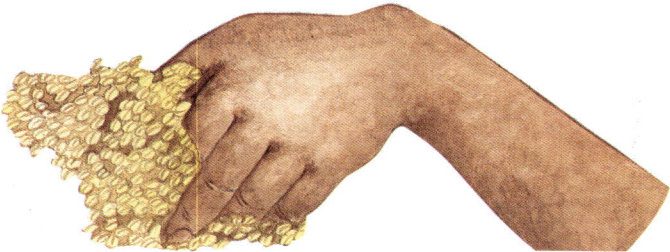

These days we no longer see
this wonderful sight
of a farmer scattering seed:
machines do the work now.

While the farmer was scattering the seed, some of it fell along the road…

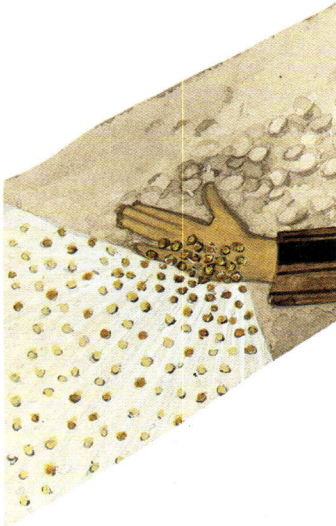

In the country where Jesus lived there were roads or paths, which crossed through the fields. As the farmer threw fistfuls of seed some of it landed on these paths instead of on the prepared ground.

There are some words that go right past our ears. We don't even hear them.

"… and was eaten by the birds."

Lucky birds!
They could easily spot the seed that landed
on the path and they gobbled it up.
They chirped merrily as they treated themselves
to a delicious meal.
But these seeds would not bear any fruit.

*Good advice can quickly disappear
if you don't take it to heart and act upon it.*

"Other seeds fell on thin, rocky ground."

The soil may be more or less all right,
but it may have stones in it.
Sometimes there are more stones than soil.
In order to grow, the seed needs soil
because it needs to keep the dampness,
which allows it to push up
through the ground.

*A lot of people have hard hearts
like the stony ground.*

*"The plants quickly started growing.
But when the sun came up, the plants were
scorched and dried up,
because they did not have
enough roots."*

Stones and rocks keep the ground warm.
Some drops of rain help the seed to grow.
But there's nowhere for it to put down roots.
Very quickly the heat from the stones makes
the scattered seed dry up and die.

*We hear a lot of words,
but there are only a few that we really listen to.*

"Some other seeds fell where thornbushes grew."

Weeds and brambles grow
more easily than good seed.
You often find them alongside paths.
Since the farmer was scattering seed
   everywhere, some of it landed among thorns.

When someone is generous,
they give without counting the cost.

"They choked the plants."

To begin with, these seeds grow well.
They feel nice and warm, protected
and sheltered from the wind
and the hungry birds.
But they have no air or light
and very soon become choked
            by the thorns.

In life, there are thorns and brambles.
They choke us and stop us
from being open to others.

"But a few seeds did fall on good ground."

To germinate (this means to grow and develop),
the seed needs light, heat and moisture.
But most of all it needs good soil
in which to put down its roots.

To live like Jesus, we have to be
like the good soil that receives his Word.

"The plants produced a hundred or sixty or thirty times as much as was scattered."

All the seed, wherever it lands,
 is of good quality.
   But it only bears fruit a hundred times
    its size if it lands on good ground.

*The seed that was sown is the Good News of Jesus;
those who welcome it will do a lot of good.*

The world is like a big field
with rocks, brambles and good soil.
Jesus generously sows his Word of love there.
Sometimes it is rejected, choked, or dug up.
But each of us can offer Jesus a patch of good soil
so that his Word can grow and bear fruit.
All Jesus' friends are given their chance
to be generous and sow the seeds of joy,
peace and love.

That same day Jesus left the house and went out beside Lake Galilee, where he sat down to teach.

"A farmer went out to sow seed in a field."

"While the farmer was scattering the seed, some of it fell along the road…"

"… and was eaten by the birds."

"Other seeds fell on thin, rocky ground."

"The plants quickly started growing. But when the sun came up, the plants were scorched and dried up, because they did not have enough roots."

"Some other seeds fell where thornbushes grew."

"They choked the plants."

"But a few seeds did fall on good ground."

"The plants produced a hundred or sixty or thirty times as much as was scattered."

IN THE SAME COLLECTIONS:

The Good Samaritan
The Paralyzed Man
Zacchaeus
On the Road to Emmaus
Bartimaeus
The Call of the Disciples
The Calming of the Storm
Shared Bread
The Prodigal Son
An Amazing Catch
The Forgiven Sinner